Level 2

Duet Favorites

by Jane Smisor Bastien

Contents

KJOS WEST · **Neil A. Kjos. Jr. Publisher** · **San Diego. California**

Forward March

Secondo

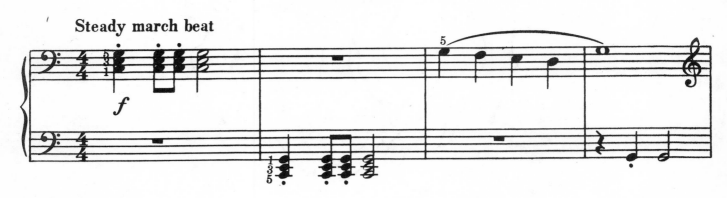

Steady march beat

Forward March

Primo

4

Shades of Blue

Secondo

Shades of Blue

Primo

Rock Along

Secondo

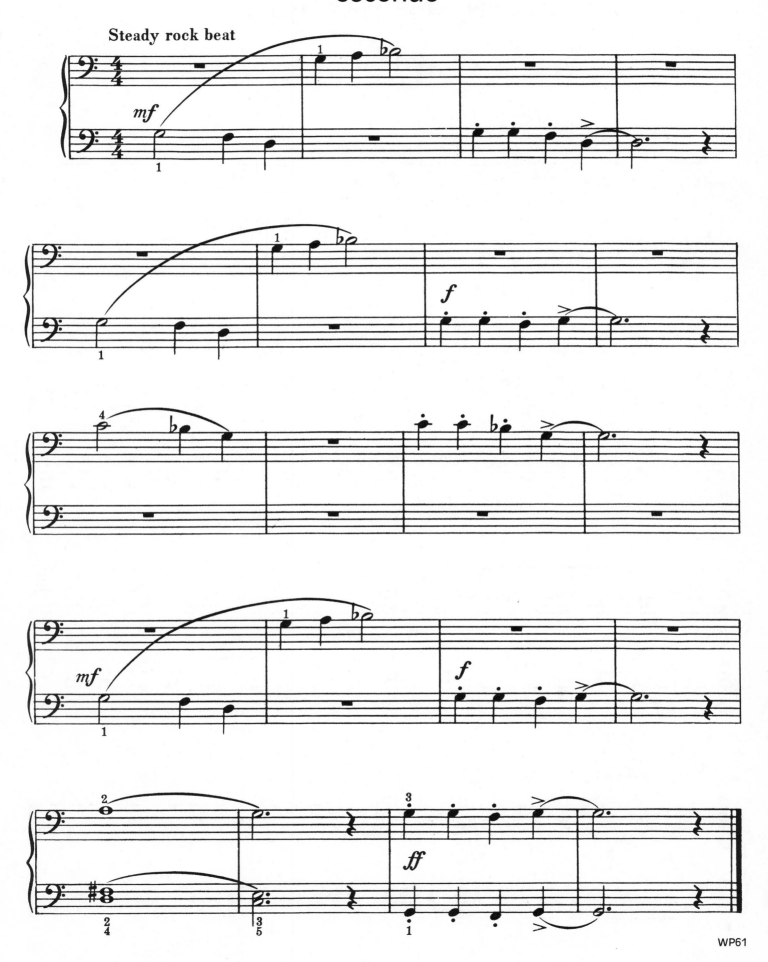

Rock Along

Primo

Old MacDonald

Secondo

Folk Song

With spirit

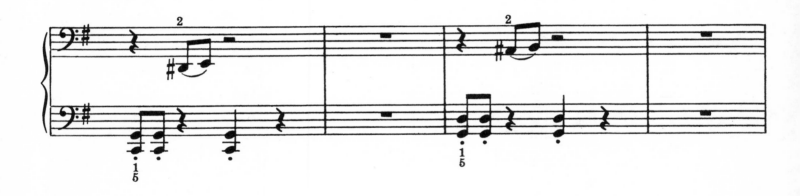

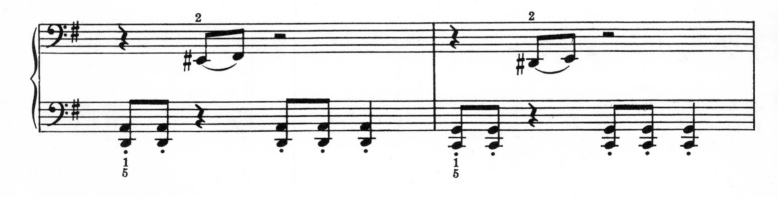

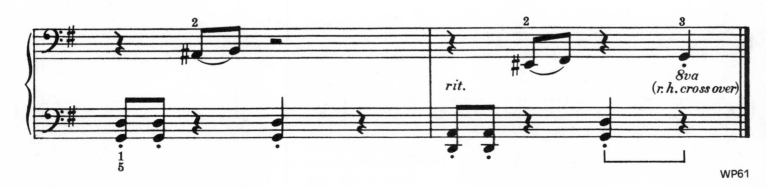

Old MacDonald

Primo

Folk Song

Carousel Tune

Secondo

Carousel Tune

Primo

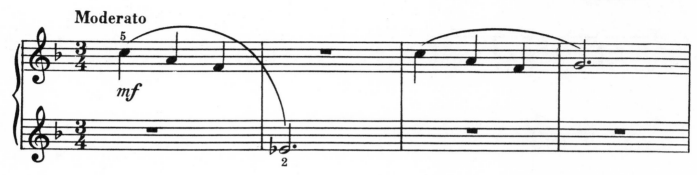

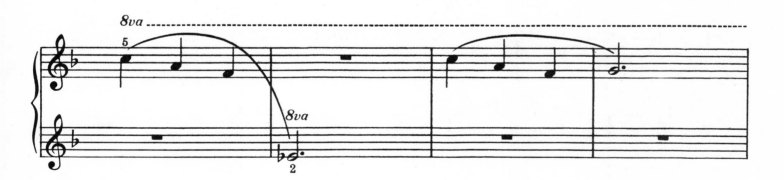

POP PIANO STYLES

A light and refreshing collection of rock, blues, boogie, and disco styles from Jane and James Bastien. From foot-stompin' rhythms to melancholy moods, these up-to-date sounds encourage practicing and performing for pianists of all ages!
Levels 1-4

Level 1
WP51

Level 2
WP52

Level 3
WP53

Level 4
WP54